HELICOPTERS

by Jeffrey Zuehlke

PULL AHEAD BOOKS
Mighty Movers

Lerner Publications Company • Minneapolis

For Geoff, my favorite high-flying buddy

Text copyright © 2005 by Lerner Publishing Group, Inc.

This book is available in two editions:
Library binding by Lerner Publications Company, a division of Lerner Publishing Group, Inc.
Soft cover by First Avenue Editions, an imprint of Lerner Publishing Group, Inc.
241 First Avenue North
Minneapolis, MN 55401 U.S.A.

Website address: www.lernerbooks.com

Library of Congress Cataloging-in-Publication Data

Zuehlke, Jeffrey, 1968–
    Helicopters / by Jeffrey Zuehlke.
        p.   cm. – (Pull ahead books)
    Includes index.
    ISBN-13: 978-0-8225-1540-1 (lib. bdg. : alk. paper)
    ISBN-10: 0-8225-1540-7 (lib. bdg. : alk. paper)
    ISBN-13: 978-0-8225-2382-6 (pbk. : alk. paper)
    ISBN-10: 0-8225-2382-5 (pbk. : alk. paper)
    1. Helicopters–Juvenile literature. [1. Helicopters.]
I. Title. II. Series.
TL716.2.Z84 2005
629.133'352–dc22   2003026937

Manufactured in the United States of America
2 3 4 5 6 7 – JR – 12 11 10 09 08 07

Whup! Whup! Whup! Whup! Whup!
What is that up in the sky?

It's a helicopter! Helicopters are amazing **aircraft.** What can they do?

They can fly high
and fast.

Helicopters can also fly low and slow.

They can
hover in one
spot in the air.

Hovering helicopters can land in small spaces. This helicopter is landing on a ship.

Helicopters can land almost anywhere.
This helicopter is in the desert.

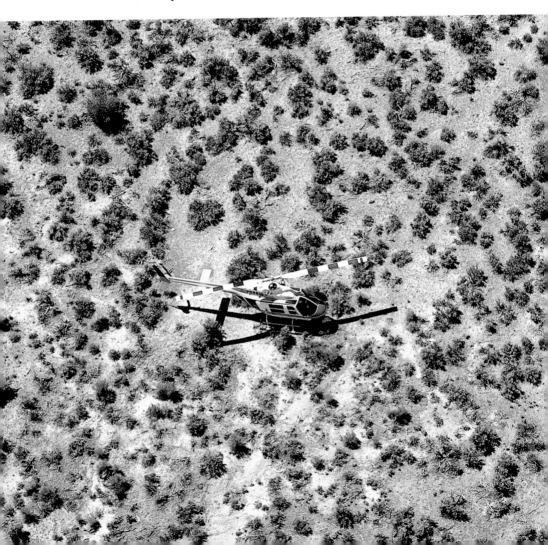

How do helicopters fly? They have special wings called **rotary wings.**

The **main rotor** turns the rotary wings.
The wings spin around fast.

The spinning
wings lift the
helicopter into
the air. But
who flies the
helicopter?

The pilot!
The pilot uses
controls to fly
the helicopter.
The controls
are in the
cockpit.

One control is the **power lever.** The power lever makes the helicopter fly up, down, or hover.

This is the **stick.** It makes the
helicopter move forward, backward, or
even sideways!

The **tail rotor** spins the tail wings.
The spinning wings turn the helicopter.

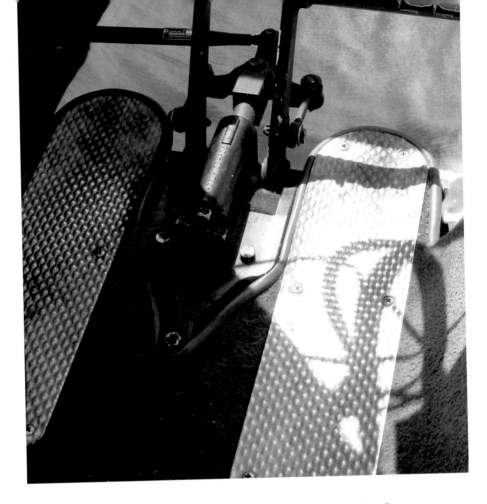

The pilot uses the **rudder pedals** to move the tail rotor.

Helicopters do special jobs. This helicopter works for the TV news.

The helicopter flies slowly over the action. The cameraperson gets a good view.

Police officers use helicopters to find suspects. Suspects are people the police think have broken a law.

This helicopter helped catch a suspect!

What else do helicopters do? Some helicopters work as ambulances.

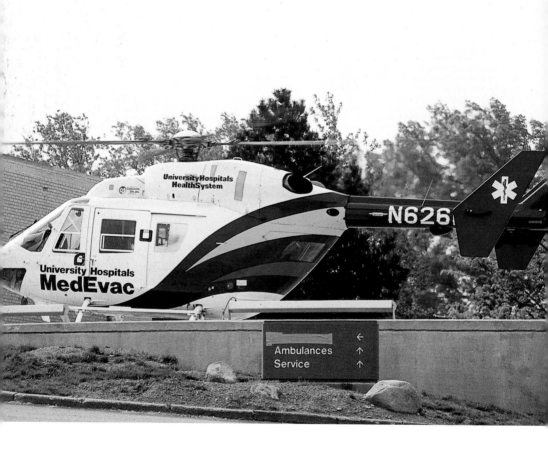

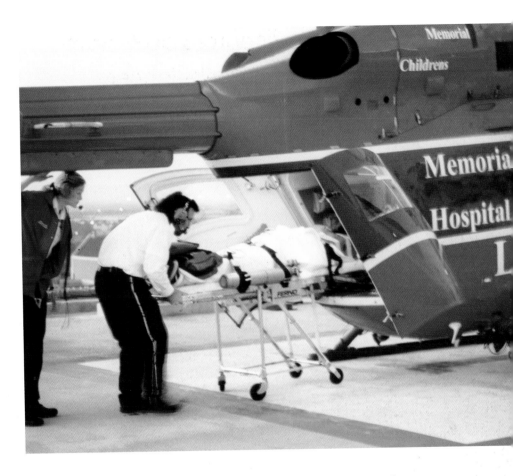

They can get people who are sick or
hurt to the hospital fast.

Helicopters help fight fires. This
helicopter is picking up some water.

Watch it dump water on the fire!

Rescue helicopters help reach lost or hurt people. See the person hanging below the helicopter?

The helicopter is lifting this person to safety. The helicopter saved the day!

Facts about Helicopters

- In 1483, an Italian inventor named Leonardo da Vinci came up with an idea for a helicopter. He drew a picture of the machine, but he never tried to build it.

- The first helicopter flight was made in 1907. The helicopter lifted two feet off the ground for about one minute.

- Helicopters have many names. They are called rotorcraft, choppers, whirlybirds, and eggbeaters.

- The fastest helicopter is the Westland Lynx. It can fly 249 miles per hour. A car on a highway moves at about 60 miles an hour.

- Large helicopters have two main rotors but no tail rotor. The main rotors work together to turn the helicopter and help it carry heavy loads.

Parts of a Helicopter

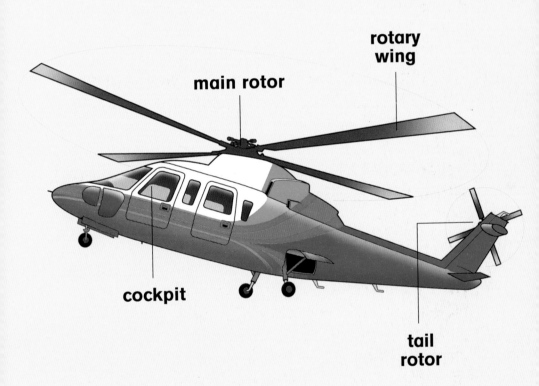

rotary wing

main rotor

cockpit

tail rotor

Glossary

aircraft: machines that can fly through the air

cockpit: the place where the pilot sits

hover: to stay in one spot in the air

main rotor: the part of a helicopter that spins the rotary wings

power lever: a lever that makes a helicopter go up, down, or hover

rotary wings: the wings on a helicopter

rudder pedals: pedals that move the tail rotor

stick: a lever that makes a helicopter go forward, backward, or sideways

tail rotor: a part that spins the tail wings

Index

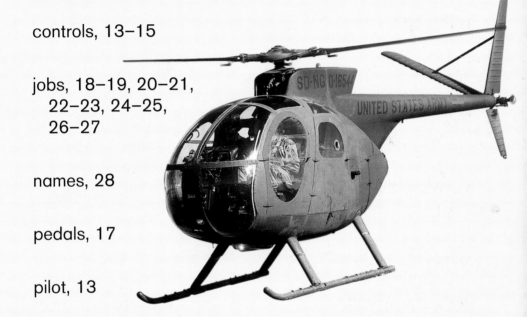

About the Author

As a kid growing up in St. Paul, Minnesota, Jeffrey Zuehlke loved to watch helicopters and airplanes flying over his house. As an adult, he spends a lot of his time at a park near his local airport. He and his dog watch the planes and whirlybirds fly past.

Photo Acknowledgments

The photographs in this book appear courtesy of: Robinson Helicopter Company, front cover; © Patrick Cone Photography, pp. 3, 5, 7, 9, 12, 13; © Charles Palek/Tom Stack and Associates, pp. 4, 31; © Artemis Images/Indianapolis Motor Speedway, p. 6; NOAA, p. 8; © The Image Finders, pp. 10, 11, 14, 15, 17; © Jim Baron/The Image Finders, pp. 16, 22; © ThinkStock/SuperStock, p. 18; © George Hall/CORBIS, p. 19, © Artemis Images/Pikes Peak International Hill Climb, p. 20; © Royalty-Free/CORBIS, pp. 21, 23; © Sardegna/La Presse/Zuma Press, pp. 24, 25; © Milton Rand/Tom Stack and Associates, p. 26; © D. Megna/Raw Talent Photography, p. 27. Illustration on p. 29 by Laura Westlund, © Lerner Publishing Group.